Roman Style

Recipes

An Illustrated Cookbook of Italian Dish Ideas!

BY

Julia Chiles

Copyright 2020 - Julia Chiles

OOOOOOOOOOOOOOOOOOOOOOOOOOOOOOOOOO

License Notes

No part of this Book can be reproduced in any form or by any means including print, electronic, scanning or photocopying unless prior permission is granted by the author.

All ideas, suggestions and guidelines mentioned here are written for informative purposes. While the author has taken every possible step to ensure accuracy, all readers are advised to follow information at their own risk. The author cannot be held responsible for personal and/or commercial damages in case of misinterpreting and misunderstanding any part of this Book

OOOOOOOOOOOOOOOOOOOOOOOOOOOOOOOO

Table of Contents

Introduction 6

Bread is heavily featured in the traditional breakfasts of Rome. Here are some tasty favorites to try........................ 8

   1 – Roman Traditional Breakfast Bread 9

   2 – Cream Filled Sweet Buns 13

   3 – Cornetti Breakfast "Rolls" 16

   4 – Ciambella Roman Breakfast Cake 19

   5 – Honey Eggs 21

Romans had and have many types of lunch, dinner, side dish and appetizer recipes that will have you wanting more. Try some soon.. 23

   6 – Linguini Clam Sauce 24

   7 – Roman Style Artichokes 27

   8 – Roman-Style Roasted Pork Loin 30

9 – Roman Alla Gricia Rigatoni 33

10 – Chicken with Fontina Prosciutto 35

11 – Traditional Peas with Prosciutto 38

12 – Traditional Roman Chicken 40

13 – Roman Spaghetti Alla Carbonara 43

14 – Marinated "Dormouse" – Chicken Drumsticks 45

15 – Traditional Wedge Salad 47

16 – Roman Roast Tuna 49

17 – Cheese with Pepper 51

18 – Fried Sweet Curd Cheese 53

19 – Traditional Summer Salad 55

20 – Garum Seasoned Mussels 57

21 – Roman-Style Egg Drop Soup 59

22 – Roman Cauliflower in Wine 61

23 – Farro Feta Cheese 64

24 – Baked Roman-Style Semolina Gnocchi 66

25 – Eggs Pine Nut Sauce 69

From ancient times through today, Rome has some intriguing and delectable desserts to offer. Try one soon... 71

26 – Ancient Romans' Cheesecake 72

27 – Traditional Holiday Granita 74

28 – Traditional Wine Cookies 76

29 – Roman Custard 78

30 – Roman Honey Cookies.. 80

Conclusion 83

Author's Afterthoughts... 85

About the Author 86

Introduction

What types of dishes are truly Roman in their origins?

Can you experience them without traveling to Italy?

Are the ingredients you will need readily available where you live?

Even though Roman cuisine utilizes many various ingredients, you can usually find them – or suitable substitutes – in most areas. They range from meats, vegetables, fruits and tempting sauces that bring them all together.

Common ingredients in Rome include sausage, ham, tomatoes and various types of cheeses. Like other Italians, Romans prefer fresh ingredients that are subtly spiced and seasoned. They use olive oil for most of their cooking, replacing the lard or animal fat used by chefs in other countries.

Of course, all of Italy is known for pasta dishes, and they are popular in Rome. They use many types of pasta, including various shapes, lengths and widths of noodles.

Some of the most commonly used pastas include lasagna, fusilli, linguine, penne and spaghetti. Pasta is sometimes filled with other tasty ingredients, as is the case with tortellini and ravioli.

There is much more to explore in Roman cooking. SO many dishes await your tasting. So today is a good day to start exploring…

Bread is heavily featured in the traditional breakfasts of Rome. Here are some tasty favorites to try...

1 – Roman Traditional Breakfast Bread

Did you know that the original Roman pizza was a breakfast recipe? This dough works for pizza, too. They didn't use tomatoes when this dish was first served, because they had none in the area at that time, but you could add a couple sun-dried tomatoes on top if you like.

Makes 2 x 9" pies

Cooking + Prep Time: 1 1/4 hour

Ingredients:
- 1 1/3 cup of water, warm
- 2 tsp. of sugar, granulated
- 1 1/2 tsp. of yeast

Optional: 2 tsp. of gluten

- 2 tbsp. of corn meal
- 1 tsp. of baking powder
- 3 cups of flour, all purpose
- 1/4 tsp. of onion powder
- 1/4 tsp. of garlic powder
- '1 tbsp. of oil, olive
- 1 tsp. of salt, kosher
- Provolone cheese
- Mozzarella cheese
- Parmesan cheese
- Toppings, meats and vegetables, your choice

Instructions:

1. Mix first three ingredients in pre-warmed bowl. Place the pan in a bread machine. Close lid and proof yeast. Allow to set for 10 to 15 minutes. Some foam should be seen on surface. This shows that yeast is active and alive. If you don't see a change, this yeast may be dead, so get a new packet. Otherwise, the water may have been too hot, and it could have killed your yeast. If this is the case, start the recipe over. If the pan happened to be too cool to activate the yeast, re-proof the yeast with warmed pan.

2. Once you have proofed the yeast, add corn meal, gluten (if using), baking powder, flour and onion and garlic powders. Place the pan in the bread machine. Begin to mix on the dough setting. Alternately, you can mix in a bowl by hand.

3. Once the ingredients are combined into a dough ball, usually five to 10 minutes or so, open the lid. Add the salt and oil. Allow the dough setting to proceed.

4. When cycle of bread machine has completed the task, preheat the oven to 425 degrees F. Remove the dough. Cut in half. Spread halves into pre-oiled pizza pans. Rub a bit of oil into your hands to help you spread the dough without it springing back at you.

5. Spread the dough halves with three cheeses and your desired toppings and bake them for 8-10 minutes or so. Raise the oven setting to the Broil setting. This will brown the crust and cheeses. Keep an eye on the loaves, as the broiler can cause them to burn swiftly. Serve.

2 – Cream Filled Sweet Buns

People who travel to Rome seldom leave without trying con la panna, or cream filled sweet buns. They are authentic and truly delicious. They are sure to fill you up and whet your appetite for sweets.

Makes 10 Servings

Cooking + Prep Time: 35 minutes + six hours of rising time

Ingredients:

- 1 1/2 tbsp. of yeast, fresh
- 1/4 cup of water, warm
- 1 pound of sifted flour, all-purpose
- 1/2 cup of sugar, granulated
- A pinch of salt, kosher
- 1 tsp. of vanilla, pure
- 4 yolks from large eggs – reserve whites
- 7 ounces of scalded milk, low fat
- 1 tsp. of cocoa powder
- 3 tbsp. of sugar, confectioner's
- 16 ounces of cream, fresh

Instructions:

1. Add yeast to the lukewarm water.

2. Sift flour into large sized bowl.

3. Add yeast/water mixture to egg yolks, sugar, milk, salt and vanilla. Stir till you have a smooth, sticky dough. This typically takes 8-10 minutes or so.

4. Transfer dough to floured plastic container (large) with a lid. Allow it to rise for four hours.

5. Line large cookie sheet with baking paper.

6. Oil your hands lightly. Form dough into balls the size of ping pong balls. Place them on cookie sheet. Gently cover with cling wrap. Allow to rise in warm area of your house for two more hours.

7. Preheat oven to 355F.

8. When dough has risen to double its size, gently brush buns with egg whites, being sure to cover the whole surface of buns.

9. Bake the buns for 20-22 minutes. Then remove them and allow to cool on wire rack.

10. Measure cream and confectioner's sugar in large sized bowl. Use a whip to whisk for five minutes, till it has become whipped cream.

11. Slice buns across their tops. Fill the gaps with the whipped cream you just made. Use cocoa powder and additional confectioner's sugar to top. Serve.

3 - Cornetti Breakfast "Rolls"

Traditional cornetti are made with methods no longer used today. This is a home version, which you may enjoy making. Enjoy them with morning coffee or cappuccino.

Makes 8 Servings

Cooking + Prep Time: 1 hour 20 minutes

Ingredients:

- 2 cups of sifted flour, all-purpose
- 1 cup of room temp. butter, unsalted
- 1 tsp. of vanilla, pure
- 8 oz. of yogurt, vanilla
- 1/2 pkg. of yeast, powdered
- Sugar, powdered
- Apricot marmalade or jam

Instructions:

1. Place butter, flour, vanilla, yogurt, pinch of salt yeast in food processor. Blend the ingredients together till they form a firm dough.

2. Place the dough on lightly floured board. Then work the dough, forming it into a round, long oval shape. Divide the oval in six separate pieces. Roll pieces out till they all have a 10" diameter. Divide those pieces into eight triangles each.

3. Spread 1 tsp. of apricot jam in middle of all triangles. Roll into croissant shapes. Pinch the ends closed.

4. Place the cornetti on cookie sheet lined with parchment paper. Bake at 375F for 18-20 minutes. Remove from oven. When cornetti have cooled, dust them using powdered sugar. Serve.

4 - Ciambella Roman Breakfast Cake

This Roman cake is made by dousing its fried dough in sugar crystals. This adds wonderful sweetness and a pleasing crunch. These pastries are fluffy and golden, and nearly irresistible.

Makes 12 Servings

Cooking + Prep Time: 45 minutes

Ingredients:

- 13 oz. of flour, all-purpose
- 5 oz. of butter, unsalted
- 6 oz. of sugar, granulated
- A pinch of salt, kosher
- 4 eggs, large
- 1 tsp. of vanilla, pure
- 1 tsp. of baking powder
- 2 tbsp. of maraschino liqueur or similar flavor
- 1 zest from orange or lemon
- 1/3 cup of milk, whole
- 1 or 2 tbsp. of sugar to top

Instructions:

1. Preheat oven to 425F.

2. Grease mold of your choice. Dust it well using flour.

3. Work all ingredients except topping sugar with kneading machine till you have a smooth batter.

4. Spread batter in your mold and top it with the sugar.

5. Bake in 425F oven for 1/2 hour. Serve.

5 – Honey Eggs

Whether you enjoy savory or sweet tastes, this nutritious, delicious breakfast is so easy to prepare. It's as simple as including the incredible egg with the sweetness of honey.

Makes 2-3 Servings

Cooking + Prep Time: 25 minutes

Ingredients:

- 4 eggs, large
- 3 tbsp. of honey, pure
- 9 1/3 fluid ounces of milk, low fat
- 3/4 oz. of butter, unsalted
- 1 tbsp. of oil, olive
- 1 pinch pepper, black, ground

Instructions:

1. Beat oil, eggs and milk together.

2. Pour a bit of oil in fry pan. Heat it up. As it sizzles, add omelet mixture from step 1.

3. Use fork to whisk till mix begins solidifying.

4. When omelet is cooked well on first side, flip and cook second side. Fold omelet in half. Place on plate.

5. Warm honey. Pour it over omelet. Fold over another time. Cut in thick slices. Then sprinkle with ground pepper. Serve.

Romans had and have many types of lunch, dinner, side dish and appetizer recipes that will have you wanting more. Try some soon...

6 – Linguini Clam Sauce

In the early days of Rome, fish was commonly served, since it was easier to access than many meats. Today, busy Romans appreciate this recipe because it can be easily made almost anytime, and many of the ingredients are readily found in their pantries.

Makes 4 Servings

Cooking + Prep Time: 1/2 hour

Ingredients:

- 1/3 cup of oil, olive
- 1 tbsp. of butter, unsalted
- 1 pound of linguine
- 6 fillets, anchovy
- 4 minced garlic cloves
- 1 pinch of crushed pepper flakes, red
- 1 lemon, juice zest only
- 1/2 tsp. of oregano, dried
- 1/4 cup of dry wine, white
- 1 1/2 cups of juice, clam
- 1 1/4 cups of drained, canned clams
- 1/2 cup of whipping cream, heavy
- 2 tbsp. of minced parsley, fresh

Instructions:

1. Cook the linguine using directions on package. Set it aside.

2. Heat oil butter in large sized skillet. Add garlic, anchovies pepper flakes. Stir while cooking till the anchovies have melted, usually one minute or so.

3. Add the lemon zest and juice, then clam juice, oregano and wine. Bring to boil and stir occasionally for seven to eight minutes.

4. Add whipping cream and clams. Heat fully through and toss with the linguine. Use parsley to garnish and serve.

7 – Roman Style Artichokes

This recipe is also known as Artichokes Alla Romana. Once you have tried them, you won't want to eat artichokes any other way. These are sautéed lovingly with olive oil, and served with garlic, oregano and mint. They are a truly tasty side or appetizer.

Makes 4 Servings

Cooking + Prep Time: 45 minutes

Ingredients:

- 10 artichokes, small or medium sized, tender
- 2 tbsp. of chopped pint, fresh
- 2 chopped garlic cloves
- 2 tsp. of oregano, dried
- 3/4 tsp. of salt, kosher
- 1/4 cup of oil, olive
- 1 cup of water, filtered

Instructions:

1. Squeeze lemon juice into large sized bowl of water. Remove outer artichoke leaves (there are usually three or four layers of them). Stop when you reach pale yellow leaves. You can keep the leaves whole or slice in halves.

2. Cut stem from artichokes. Leave two to three inches, then clean, peeling off outer layer. Place clean artichokes and their stems in the bowl of lemon water. It will prevent them from becoming brown. Set the artichokes aside.

3. Mix oil, salt, oregano, garlic and mint in small sized bowl. Drain the artichokes their stems. Place them in fry pan and cover with the oil mixture. Add one cup water. Gently mix and combine.

4. Next, cover pan. Cook on med-low heat for about 20 minutes or so. Water should have evaporated and the artichokes should be tender. Serve.

8 – Roman-Style Roasted Pork Loin

Even in her early days, the dishes of Rome utilized an impressive combination of herbs and spices. This recipe uses sage, fennel and rosemary, and the flavor hearkens back to an ancient Italian passion for food that is well-made and well-seasoned.

Makes 5-7 Servings

Cooking + Prep Time: 3 hours 20 minutes

Ingredients:

- 4 garlic cloves
- 2 tbsp. of rosemary, fresh
- 2 tbsp. of sage leaves, fresh
- 4 tbsp. of oil, olive
- 2 tsp. of fennel seeds
- 1 x 5-pound pork loin roast, bone-in
- Salt, sea
- Pepper, ground
- 1 sliced onion, medium
- 1 cup of dry wine, white
- 1 tbsp. of butter, unsalted

Instructions:

1. Preheat the oven to 325F.

2. Mince fennel seeds, sage, rosemary and garlic in your food processor. Rub pork using 2 tbsp. oil. Rub herb mixture on roast. Season using sea salt ground pepper.

3. Transfer pork to roasting pan. Leave pan uncovered and roast for an hour. Toss onion and remainder of oil. Add mixture to pan. Continue to roast till internal pork temperature is 160F. This takes about an hour and a half. Transfer roast to platter. Use foil to loosely cover. Allow to rest for 15-18 minutes.

4. Place roasting pan on med. heat. Add wine. Stir and scrape up bits from bottom. Simmer till sauce has been reduced a bit. Whisk in the butter. Carve roast. Serve along with sauce from pan.

9 – Roman Alla Gricia Rigatoni

Here is a dish commonly served in the restaurants of Rome, but you can make it at home, too. There are several versions of the origin, but it is undeniably delicious in any version.

Makes 4 Servings

Cooking + Prep Time: 45 minutes

Ingredients:

- 6 oz. of guanciale cured meat
- 1 lb. of rigatoni
- 1/4 lb. of grated Pecorino Romano
- Black pepper, ground

Optional: 1 chopped onion, small 1/2 cup of wine, white

Instructions:

1. Slice guanciale into thick slices. Cut those slices into 1/3" wide chunks.

2. Toss guanciale chunks in hot pan till fat has melted meat begins to brown.

3. Add the onion wine if you're using them. Allow wine to mostly evaporate and turn off flame. Cook rigatoni per **Instructions** on package. Add to the pan.

4. Mix rigatoni quickly in pan till pasta is moist with the fat.

5. Divide on plates. Use pecorino and pepper to sprinkle. Serve.

10 – Chicken with Fontina Prosciutto

This recipe can be varied by making it using Swiss cheese, ham, oregano, tomato sauce, mozzarella cheese, pepperoni and herbs. Indeed, many combinations of meats, cheese and herbs will work just as well. You can either stuff the chicken before you sauté it or do the sautéing first. Many chefs prefer to sauté first so they don't lose as much filling while cooking.

Makes 4 Servings

Cooking + Prep Time: 55 minutes

Ingredients:

- 4 fillets, chicken
- 2 tbsp. of butter, unsalted
- 2 tbsp. of oil, olive
- 4 slices of prosciutto cured ham
- 4 slices of cheese, Fontina
- 4 leaves of basil
- Salt, kosher
- Pepper, ground
- 1/2 cup of dry wine, white

Instructions:

1. Preheat the oven to 400F.

2. Use non-stick spray to coat a casserole dish. Slice lengthways slits in fillets, forming pockets.

3. Melt oil and butter in large sized skillet. Sauté the chicken fillets till they are a golden-brown color on each side.

4. Open fillets. Layer them with cheese, prosciutto leaves of basil. Close the fillets and season them using kosher salt ground pepper.

5. Transfer fillets to casserole dish. Add the wine. Leave dish uncovered and bake for 18-20 minutes, till chicken has cooked through with no pink remaining. The cheese should be melted, too. Remove from oven and serve.

11 – Traditional Peas with Prosciutto

Also known as piselli alla romana, this elegant and tasty side dish is a very simple recipe. Almost anyone could make it, and it will always have a tempting, appealing taste.

Makes 4-6 Servings

Cooking + Prep Time: 20 minutes

Ingredients:

- Oil, olive
- 1/2 chopped onion, medium
- 1 x 16-ounce bag of peas, frozen or 16 oz. of fresh peas, shelled
- 2 or 3 prosciutto slices, thin-strip sliced
- Kosher salt
- Ground pepper

Instructions:

1. Sweat onions in oil till they are translucent. Add thin cross-grain cut prosciutto strips. Continue to cook till prosciutto doesn't look "raw" anymore.

2. Add the peas and stir well. Allow peas to absorb flavors in pan while cooking. Allow peas to simmer till they are tender, usually 18-20 minutes or so. Season as desired. Serve.

12 – Traditional Roman Chicken

This dish is an especially perfect one for sharing. The chicken thighs and breasts, prosciutto, vegetables, tomatoes herbs create such an enticing recipe.

Makes 4 Servings

Cooking + Prep Time: 1 hour 10 minutes

Ingredients:

- 4 rib-in halved chicken breasts, skinless
- 2 bone-in chicken thighs, skinless
- 1/2 tsp. + 1 tsp. of salt, kosher
- 1/2 tsp. + 1 tsp. of pepper, ground
- 1/4 cup of oil, olive
- 1 sliced bell pepper, red
- 2 sliced bell peppers, yellow
- 3 ounces of sliced prosciutto
- 2 chopped garlic cloves
- 1 x 15-ounce can of diced tomatoes
- 1/2 cup of wine, white
- 1 tbsp. of thyme leaves, fresh
- 1 tsp. of oregano leaves, fresh
- 1/2 cup of stock, chicken
- 1/4 cup of chopped parsley leaves, flat leaf, fresh
- 2 tbsp. of capers

Instructions:

1. Season chicken using 1/2 tsp. each kosher salt ground pepper. In large, heavy skillet, heat oil on med. heat. When oil becomes hot, cook chicken till browned on each side. Remove chicken from skillet. Set it aside.

2. Add prosciutto and peppers to same skillet, still on med. heat. Cook till prosciutto becomes crisp and peppers are browned, five minutes or so. Add garlic. Cook for one minute. Then add wine, tomatoes herbs. Scrape browned bits from bottom of skillet with wooden spoon.

3. Return chicken to skillet. Add stock. Bring mixture to boil. Lower heat. Cover skillet and simmer till chicken has cooked fully through with no pink, usually 20-30 minutes or so.

4. Add parsley and capers. Serve.

13 – Roman Spaghetti Alla Carbonara

This is a dish that has always been popular with the people of Rome. It includes pasta, eggs and pecorino. It's a high-protein dish, thanks to the meat and eggs.

Makes 4 Servings

Cooking + Prep Time: 35 minutes

Ingredients:

- 8 oz. of diced guanciale cured meat
- 1 lb. of spaghetti
- 2 eggs, large
- 1 cup of grated Pecorino Romano

Instructions:

1. Fry guanciale in large sized pan on med-high till crisp and rendered, 10 minutes or so.

2. Use fork to beat pecorino and eggs together in small sized bowl. Set it aside.

3. Cook spaghetti till al dente. Drain and return to the pot. Toss with rendered fat and guanciale on low heat. Transfer promptly to bowls.

4. Pour the cheese and egg mixture over bowls. Add pepper as desired. Mix quickly to use hot pasta to cook eggs slightly. You want a creamy texture. Serve.

14 - Marinated "Dormouse" - Chicken Drumsticks

Romans in ancient times ate "dormouse", which was a rodent that would destroy crops, so they needed to be eradicated. They then became a delicacy. The dormouse is not found easily today, and this recipe is more palatable for many people, since it uses chicken drumsticks. Be sure to marinate them overnight for the best flavor.

Makes 8 drumsticks

Cooking + Prep Time: 55 minutes + overnight refrigeration time

Ingredients:

- 8 drumsticks, chicken
- 1 cup of flour, all-purpose
- 2 tsp. of paprika powder, sweet
- 2 tsp. of caraway seeds
- 2 tsp. of cumin seeds
- 1 tbsp. of honey, pure
- 2 bay leaves, fresh
- A bit of oil, vegetable

Instructions:

1. Crush cumin seeds. Pour flour into plastic bag with caraway seeds, cumin, paprika and bay leaves.

2. Dab some oil lightly on drumsticks. Toss in bag with flour mixture. Add honey to bag. Swirl bag and set in refrigerator overnight to allow sinking in of flavors.

3. Next day, put drumsticks in oiled pan. Bake for 20 to 30 minutes, till skewer inserted in thickest area of meat will only release clear juice. Remove from oven and serve.

15 - Traditional Wedge Salad

When you are faced with tackling and enjoying a wedge salad, the simplest way is by chopping it up and tossing it all on your plate, together. In this way, each layer of tomatoes and lettuce will become coated with the tasty dressing, and you'll get pancetta in almost every bite.

Makes 3-4 Servings

Cooking + Prep Time: 20 minutes

Ingredients:

- 1/4 lb. of pancetta cured meat
- 2 tsp. of oil, olive
- 1/2 head of lettuce, large
- 2 sliced tomatoes
- 2 cups of dressing, blue cheese
- 1/2 cup of blue cheese, crumbled

Instructions:

1. Unroll pancetta. Chop in small sized pieces.

2. Heat the oil in med. pan till hot. Then add the pancetta. Cook on med. heat till it is crispy. Drain it on a plate with paper towels. Discard fat.

3. Slice 1/2 head of lettuce in 3-4 wedges. Arrange them on individual salad plates. Then arrange the sliced tomatoes around lettuce wedges.

4. Pour the dressing over lettuce wedges. Sprinkle with crispy pancetta on top, then with blue cheese crumbles. Serve promptly.

16 – Roman Roast Tuna

This roasted dish is a common way that fish were prepared in the ancient days of Rome. The best season for catching fresh tuna is between June and November. They made use of all parts of the tuna, as well.

Makes 2 3 Servings

Cooking + Prep Time: 25 minutes

Ingredients:

- 2 tuna steaks, large
- Vinaigrette dressing, bottled
- 3 tbsp. of vinegar, strong
- 2 tbsp. of garum fish sauce
- 1 cup of oil, olive
- 4 shallots, chopped finely
- 1 tsp. of pepper, ground
- 1 tsp. of celery seeds
- 1 bunch of mint, fresh
- For garnishing: olives

Instructions:

1. Brush fillets using oil, kosher salt ground pepper.

2. Grill on one side on hot grill.

3. Turn and brush grilled side using dressing. Repeat.

4. Don't allow the tuna to overcook. You want pink flesh inside.

5. Garnish with olives. Serve with rest of dressing.

17 – Cheese with Pepper

Also known as Cacio e Pepe, this dish is quick enough to be prepared for dinner on weeknights. There are very few ingredients needed, and the exquisite simplicity is typical of Roman meals.

Makes 4-6 Servings

Cooking + Prep Time: 20 minutes

Ingredients:

- 1 pound of long pasta, like spaghetti
- 1/2 pound of pecorino cheese, grated
- Pepper, black, ground
- Salt, kosher, for pasta water

Instructions:

1. Boil pasta in salted water. Then drain and pour into warmed, large sized bowl.

2. Add pecorino and plenty of pepper. Mix well till hot water clinging to pasta is melting the cheese. This creates a nice, creamy sauce.

3. Top with more pecorino and pepper, if desired. Serve.

18 – Fried Sweet Curd Cheese

The curd cheese used in this recipe is somewhat similar to typical cream cheese, but it has less fat. It has a lighter color and texture, too. You can also use ricotta for this dish.

Makes various # Servings

Cooking + Prep Time: 30 minutes + 3-4 hours dough setting time

Ingredients:

- 1 pound of curd cheese
- Honey, pure
- 1 cup of semolina
- Oil, olive

Instructions:

1. Drain cheese. Squeeze out excess moisture with colander or sieve.

2. Mix cheese and semolina into loose dough. Allow it to sit for three to four hours or so.

3. Wet your hands and form dough into dumplings. Fry them quickly in oil for several minutes.

4. Drain dumplings. Roll them in honey. Serve.

19 – Traditional Summer Salad

When you have friends to your house for a summer barbeque, this salad is an excellent side dish to accompany hamburgers, hot dogs, steak, etc. It's simple to make and tomato lovers will enjoy it most of all.

Makes 4 Servings

Cooking + Prep Time: 55 minutes

Ingredients:

- 1 cup of vinegar, balsamic
- 1 cup of halved black green olives, pitted
- 1/4 cup of chopped parsley leaves, fresh
- 3 drained, chopped anchovy fillets
- 2 tbsp. of rinsed, drained capers
- 1 sliced clove of garlic
- 8 shredded basil leaves, fresh
- 1/2 tsp. of pepper, ground
- 6 tbsp. of oil, olive
- 3 tomatoes, vine-ripened

Instructions:

1. Cook vinegar in small pan on low heat till it is syrupy and thick and reduced to 1/4 of a cup. This takes 18-20 minutes or so. Set it aside so it can cool.

2. Combine oil, pepper, basil, garlic, capers, anchovies, parsley and olives in small sized bowl. Combine by tossing.

3. Slice tomatoes and place overlapped on serving platter. Spoon olive/parsley mixture on top. Drizzle with balsamic dressing. Serve.

20 – Garum Seasoned Mussels

The Roman empire spanned the Mediterranean Sea on two sides, so they had seafood feasts quite often. They sometimes salted, smoked or pickled fish, and even used honey to preserve it. This mussel recipe, however, just requires simple cooking.

Makes 4 Servings

Cooking + Prep Time: 25 minutes

Ingredients:

- 40 to 50 mussels, ready to wash
- 1/2 cup of Italian dessert wine
- 2 tbsp. of garum fish sauce, bottled
- 1/2 cup of wine
- 1 chopped leek
- 1 handful minced cumin, fresh

Instructions:

1. Wash mussels well and make sure all sand has been removed.

2. Fill a pan with water sufficient to fully cover mussels. Add mussels and boil with remainder of ingredients. Serve.

21 – Roman-Style Egg Drop Soup

This is an easy soup to make, and it will warm you up nicely. That is one of the main ideals of Italian cooking. You will whisk cheese and egg into slow cooked broth, and the taste is that of a simple but supportive comfort food.

Makes 4 Servings

Cooking + Prep Time: 1/2 hour

Ingredients:

- 4 eggs, large
- 1/4 cup of grated Parmesan cheese
- 1/4 tsp. of pepper, ground
- 1/4 tsp. of nutmeg, ground
- 8 cups of broth from bollito di manzo meat soup

Instructions:

1. Whisk pepper, nutmeg, cheese and eggs into one cup of cold broth.

2. Bring the rest of broth to boil in medium sized pan. Add egg mixture while constantly whisking. Reduce the heat. Simmer for a minute while still whisking. Season as desired. Serve.

22 – Roman Cauliflower in Wine

This may be one of the best-tasting cauliflower dishes you've ever had. It is filled with tangy, bright flavors, including garlic and red wine, which punch up its taste. It's healthy, too!

Makes 8+ Servings

Cooking + Prep Time: 50 minutes

Ingredients:

- 1 cauliflower head
- 2 tbsp. of oil, olive
- 1/2 cup of dry wine, red
- 2 minced garlic cloves
- 1/4 cup of pecorino Romano, grated
- Salt, kosher
- Pepper, ground

Instructions:

1. Rinse off cauliflower. Trim all florets off.

2. Heat oil on med-low. Sauté the cauliflower for two minutes or so. Add the garlic. Sauté till it has softened, but is not yet brown, one minute or so.

3. Add wine. Cover pot and simmer for 15-17 minutes, till cauliflower has softened somewhat.

4. Remove cover from pan. Raise heat and stir constantly till wine has all evaporated.

5. Remove the pan from stove top burner. Place the cauliflower in serving dish. Then add cheese, kosher salt ground pepper as desired. Mix well. Serve.

23 – Farro Feta Cheese

This grain dish was likely a meal for the poorer citizens of Rome, in ancient times. The recipe may make a kale lover out of you. Although this recipe includes tomatoes, it would have been made without tomatoes in the early days of the Roman empire, since they were not seen on the Italian peninsula that early.

Makes 4 Servings

Cooking + Prep Time: 25 minutes

Ingredients:

- 1 cup of farro, uncooked
- 1 can of drained garbanzo beans
- 2 cups of baby kale or baby spinach
- 1 cup of halved tomatoes, grape
- 2 tbsp. of lemon juice, fresh
- 1 minced garlic clove
- Pepper, ground, as desired
- 1/4 cup of oil, olive
- 1/2 cup of crumbled feta cheese

Instructions:

1. Cook the farro using the instructions on the package.

2. Combine the farro with tomatoes, garbanzo beans and greens in large sized bowl.

3. Mix oil, lemon juice, garlic and pepper in small sized bowl. Pour it over the farro and tomato mixture. Use feta cheese to top and serve.

24 – Baked Roman-Style Semolina Gnocchi

Outside Italy, most people are familiar with small and tender gnocchi. In Rome, they eat a different kind. It's flat and round and made using semolina flour and served with butter and cheese.

Makes 4 Servings

Cooking + Prep Time: 50 minutes

Ingredients:

- 3 eggs, large
- 8 ounces of semolina
- 1 1/2 pints of milk, low fat
- 2 1/2 oz. of cheese, parmesan or asiago
- 2 1/2 oz. of grated pecorino
- 2 1/2 oz. of chopped butter, unsalted

Instructions:

1. Beat eggs in medium bowl. Add semolina. Combine thoroughly. Add milk gradually whisk till incorporated well.

2. Place mixture in large sized sauce pan on med. heat. Constantly stir for five minutes or so, till thickened.

3. Add asiago cheese and 1/2 of pecorino. Season as desired. Remove from heat. Residual heat in pan will finish melting cheese. Combine by stirring. Turn onto cookie sheet lined with cling wrap.

4. Pat mixture to 3/4-inch thickness. Chill till completely cool.

5. Preheat oven to 400F.

6. Dot 1/2 butter on base of oven-proof dish. Then cut out circles of 1 1/2 – 2 inches from firmed semolina. You can use a glass or cookie cutter. Arrange circles on base of dish. Overlap them slightly. Dot the rest of the butter over them. Sprinkle with remaining pecorino.

7. Bake for 20-25 minutes, till golden in color and serve hot.

25 – Eggs Pine Nut Sauce

Eggs are among the most popular of Roman appetizers. In this recipe, the pine sauce accents the eggs sublimely.

Makes 2-4 Servings

Cooking + Prep Time: 10 minutes + 3 to 4 hours pine nut soaking time

Ingredients:

- 4 eggs, med-boiled
- 3 tbsp. of vinegar
- 2 oz. of pine nuts
- 1 tsp. of honey, pure
- 1 pinch each celery leaf and pepper, ground

Instructions:

1. Soak pine nuts in vinegar for three to four hours before you start making sauce.

2. Mix sauce ingredients well in food processor.

3. Pour sauce into sauce boat so everyone can serve themselves over your main dish.

From ancient times through today, Rome has some intriguing and delectable desserts to offer. Try one soon...

26 – Ancient Romans' Cheesecake

If you're invited to a toga-themed party, this cheesecake will let you take along one authentic dish. This is nothing like the cheesecake you see in New York. You can serve this cheesecake cold or warm.

Makes 8 Servings

Cooking + Prep Time: 50 minutes

Ingredients:

- Water, filtered
- 15 bay leaves, fresh
- 3 eggs, large
- 8 oz. of cheese, ricotta
- 1/2 cup of honey, organic
- 1 tsp. of orange zest, grated
- 1 tsp. of juice, lemon
- 1/2 cup of flour, all-purpose

Instructions:

1. Preheat oven to 425F. Pour filtered water into small sized, ovenproof bowl. Place in oven. Arrange bay leaves covering bottom of a springform pan.

2. Beat eggs in medium bowl. Add and mix in the ricotta, orange zest, lemon juice and honey. Sprinkle flour in stir till combined evenly. Pour batter gently over bay leaves without disturbing them.

3. Bake in 425F oven till it browns, usually 35-40 minutes or so. Run knife tip around pan edges to release from pan. Invert on serving plate. May be serve chilled or warm.

27 – Traditional Holiday Granita

This dessert boasts a heavenly coffee aroma that will surround you and entice you until you give in and partake. The refreshing confection is usually served in plastic cups except at holiday gatherings, when glass mugs are often used.

Makes 4 Servings

Cooking + Prep Time: 1 hour 10 minutes

Ingredients:

- 1 cup of coffee, freshly brewed
- 1/4 cup of blood orange or tangerine juice, freshly squeezed
- 4 tsp. of sugar, granulated
- 1/2 cup of whipping cream, light

Instructions:

1. Mix coffee, sugar and citrus juice together and combine well. Then transfer mixture to a glass loaf pan. Place in freezer.

2. Allow mixture to crystallize in freezer, which usually takes about 1/2 hour. Begin scraping with palette knife or fork to break it up.

3. Place loaf pan back in freezer for 20 more minutes and scrape to break apart again. Repeat these steps for a little over one hour. You want crystallized coffee shards.

4. Whip cream with whisk. Spoon granita into martini glasses or glass mugs. Top with the cream and serve.

28 - Traditional Wine Cookies

If you are tired of all the desserts that sometimes taste TOO sweet, these wine cookies may be just what you're hungry for. They are not exactly biscotti – they are more like biscuits and are not as sweet. You can eat them alone or dip in coffee or milk.

# of servings varies by size

Cooking + Prep Time: 55 minutes

Ingredients:

- 1/2 cup of wine, dry, red or white
- 1/2 cup of oil, canola
- 1/2 cup of sugar, granulated
- 1/4 tsp. of salt, kosher
- 2 cups of flour, all-purpose

Instructions:

1. Preheat the oven to 350F.

2. Combine the oil, wine, salt and sugar well in bowl.

3. Gradually add the flour and stir to combine well, till dough has come together and is starting to hold its own shape. You can use your hands to knead if you need to, till flour is fully incorporated.

4. Roll the dough into 1/2" balls and then into 3" long cylinder. Connect ends, creating the shape of a donut.

5. If you want a sweeter taste, sprinkle with or dip in extra sugar.

6. Place on cookie sheet. Bake for 20 to 25 minutes, till browned lightly. Serve.

29 – Roman Custard

The people of ancient Rome did make custard, similar to the way we do now, but they didn't have vanilla yet, so they used honey. It's still made that way today and it's totally delicious.

Makes 8 Servings

Cooking + Prep Time: 55 minutes

Ingredients:

- 2 cups of milk, low fat
- 5 eggs, large
- 1/4 cup of honey, pure

Instructions:

1. Whisk the milk honey together in med. bowl till blended completely.

2. In separate, medium bowl, whisk the eggs till they are frothy.

3. Combine the eggs and the milk mixture. Blend thoroughly.

4. Pour batter into 11" x 7" pan. Place in 300F oven and bake for 25-35 minutes, till knife pushed into custard comes back clean. Serve.

30 – Roman Honey Cookies

These are replicas of the kind of cookies that people might have made in ancient Rome. Who knew that the Romans even ate cookies? These are not overly-authentic, but they do give you an idea of one of the sweets that early Romans snacked on.

Makes 2-4 Servings

Cooking + Prep Time: 50 minutes + 1 hour chilling time

Ingredients:

- 2 1/2 cups of flour, all-purpose
- 1 tsp. of baking powder
- 1/8 tsp. of baking soda
- 1/4 tsp. of salt, kosher
- 1/2 cup of room temperature butter, unsalted
- 1/2 cup of honey, pure
- 2 eggs, large
- 1/2 cup of sesame seeds
- Extra butter, melted

Instructions:

1. Preheat the oven to 375F. Line cookie sheets with parchment paper.

2. Combine the flour, salt, baking soda and baking powder in medium bowl. Set it aside.

3. Combine eggs, butter and honey in large sized mixer bowl. Mix well till combined fully. Beat in flour mixture gradually. Cover. Chill dough for one hour or so, till firm.

4. Form the chilled dough in one-inch balls. Place on cookie sheets. Flatten balls a bit. Bake for 10 minutes or so, till golden brown in color.

5. While cookies are still warm, remove them from cookie sheets. Brush with the melted butter. Roll them in the sesame seeds. Cool on wire rack and serve.

Conclusion

This Roman cookbook has shown you…

How to use different ingredients to affect unique Italian tastes in dishes both well-known and rare. Italian cuisine has had international acclaim for many years.

How can you include Roman dishes in your home recipes?

You can…

- Make breakfast bread (the original, tomato-less pizza), which I imagine not many people know about. Who knew pizza started out as the first meal of the day?

- Learn to cook with lettuce, cabbage, leeks, apples, pears, chestnuts and figs, which were widely used in Rome. Many are still used in authentic dishes today.

- Enjoy making the delectable seafood dishes of Rome, served in a unique fish sauce known as garum. Fish is a mainstay in the region, and there are SO many ways to make it great.

- Make dishes with dry white wine, which is often used in Italian cooking.

- Make various types of desserts like Roman custard and traditional wine cookies, which will tempt your family's sweet tooth.

Have fun experimenting! Enjoy the results!

Author's Afterthoughts

Thanks ever so much to each of my cherished readers for investing the time to read this book!

I know you could have picked from many other books, but you chose this one. So, a big thanks for reading all the way to the end. If you enjoyed this book or received value from it, I'd like to ask you for a favor. Please take a few minutes to **post an honest and heartfelt review on** *Amazon.com*. Your support does make a difference and helps to benefit other people.

Thanks!

Julia Chiles

About the Author

Julia Chiles

(1951-present)

Julia received her culinary degree from Le Counte' School of Culinary Delights in Paris, France. She enjoyed cooking more than any of her former positions. She lived in Montgomery, Alabama most of her life. She married Roger

Chiles and moved with him to Paris as he pursued his career in journalism. During the time she was there, she joined several cooking groups to learn the French cuisine, which inspired her to attend school and become a great chef.

Julia has achieved many awards in the field of food preparation. She has taught at several different culinary schools. She is in high demand on the talk show circulation, sharing her knowledge and recipes. Julia's favorite pastime is learning new ways to cook old dishes.

Julia is now writing cookbooks to add to her long list of achievements. The present one consists of favorite recipes as well as a few culinary delights from other cultures. She expands everyone's expectations on how to achieve wonderful dishes and not spend a lot of money. Julia firmly believes a wonderful dish can be prepare out of common household staples.

If anyone is interested in collecting Julia's cookbooks, check out your local bookstores and online. They are a big seller whatever venue you choose to purchase from.

Printed in the USA
CPSIA information can be obtained
at www.ICGtesting.com
CBHW031818100724
11404CB00005B/145